FRANNY'S FIX-iT SHOP

by Edward Miller

HOLIDAY HOUSE NEW YORK

Franny Fixit can fix anything.
Her robot friend, Robbie,
knows a lot, too.

3

4

Wagons and many other things are made with metals and plastics. There's only a limited supply of metal on the Earth, and someday it will run out. Wasted plastics pollute the land, air, and water and can be harmful to animals and birds. So it's better to reuse than to throw things away.

6

Friction is the slowing or stopping effect caused when one object rubs against another, otherwise known as drag.

force

friction

wheel

axle

A **Wheel and Axle** is a simple machine. When you place a heavy object on a wheel and axle and push it, the rolling of the wheels reduces the friction. When there is less friction, it takes less force to move the object.

force

friction

SCREWDRIVER

NUTS

Doorknob

Ship wheel

Bicycle wheel

wheel → axle

axle ←

axle

Plane

Truck

wheel axle

wheel axle

Rolling Pin

Wheels and axles are everywhere!

wheel axle

9

An **Inclined Plane** is a simple machine used to increase speed and raise and lower heavy objects. Ramps and slides are inclined planes.

We can go even faster on an inclined plane. The skateboard picks up speed—it accelerates.

Levers

Pliers

fulcrum

Hammer

Sure. Did you know that the blades are levers?

Stapler fulcrum

A **Lever** is a simple machine. It is a bar that pivots on a fixed point. It makes things easier to lift. A seesaw is a lever.

The **Fulcrum** is the point where the lever rests and where it pivots.

13

The blades of scissors are also wedges. The sharp edges do the cutting.

sharp edge

Close-up of the wedge-shaped edge.

14

Franny, be careful—don't cut your finger on that sharp wedge edge.

A **Wedge** is a simple machine shaped like a triangle. It's used for splitting things apart. Shovels and pushpins are wedges.

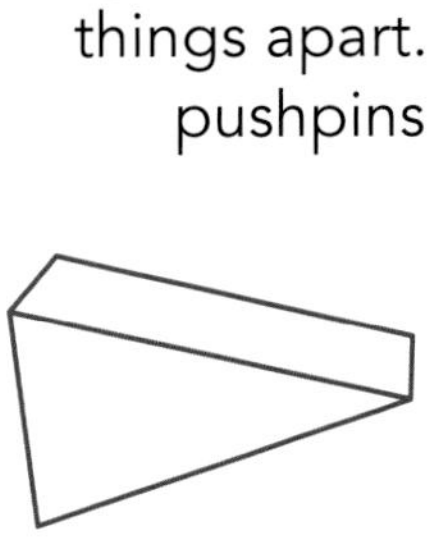

Pushpin

wedge →

Shovel

15

The scissors need a screw to hold the blades together. I have a recycled one we can use.

SCREW

A pair of scissors is three machines in one—a LEVER, a WEDGE, and a SCREW.

SCREWS

SCREW bottom

SCREW top

SCREW top

Water

Peanut Butter

You did it, Franny!

Screws hold me together.

A **SCREW** is a simple machine. It's used for holding things together. Large screws are used for digging holes.

LOOK closely at a screw and you'll see an inclined plane wrapped around the cylinder, called a thread.

Gears are simple machines. They are wheels with teeth that interlock. They are used in machines to increase power and speed.

18

Oh, I see the problem—the chain fell off the gears. I can put it back.

Oh, that's why it won't go.

Chain

Gear

Gear

Wheel

Crank

Pedal

On a go-kart, two gears are connected by a chain. One gear is attached to a crank, and the other one is attached to the back wheel. When you pedal, these parts spin the back wheel, moving the machine forward.

A **PULLEY** is a wheel and axle with a chain around it. When you pull down on the chain, the wheel spins. It's used to move things up and down.

Wheel →

Axle

Chain

Franny, could you fix my bike, too? It's not running so well.

Sure, I'll take it to my shop and see what I can do.

A bicycle is a compound machine. It has screws, gears, a pulley, levers, and wheels working together. It has many moving parts.

Chain & Gears (Pulley)

Gear →

Crank & Pedal (Lever)

Screws (all over the bicycle)

22

A **Compound machine** is a machine made up of two or more simple machines.

Handlebars
(Lever)

Brakes
(Lever)

Head tube
(Inclined Plane)

Brakes
(Lever)

Wheel

Axle

People-powered vehicles such as bicycles, tricycles, and scooters are good for the environment. They use energy from people to move instead of fuels from the Earth such as gasoline.

I replaced the missing fender.

I pumped air into the tires.

I checked the brakes to make sure the bike is safe to ride.

LOVE

CITY HALL

Wheels & Axles

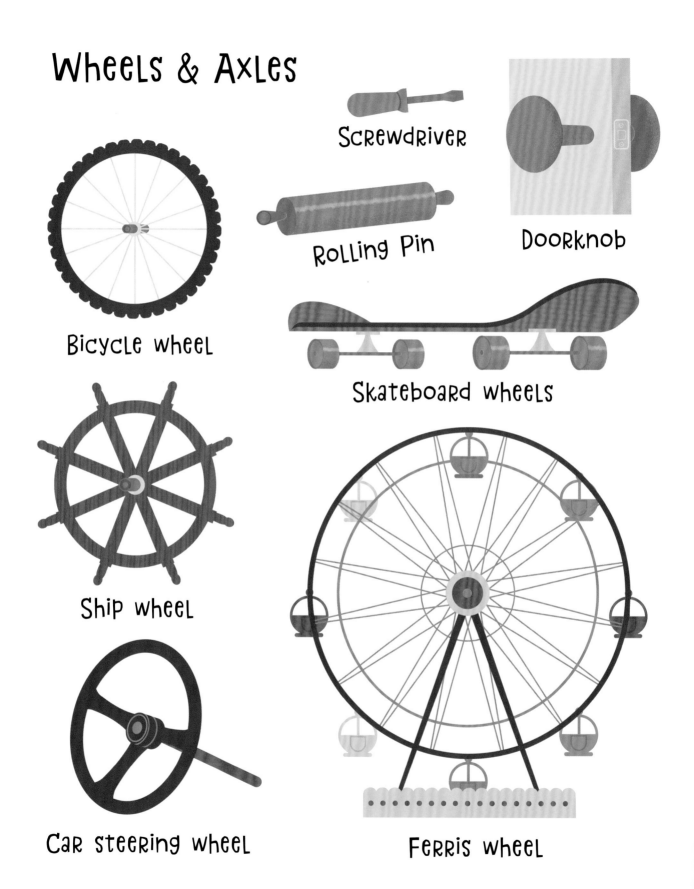

Screwdriver

Doorknob

Rolling Pin

Bicycle wheel

Skateboard wheels

Ship wheel

Car steering wheel

Ferris wheel

SCREWS

inclined plane

Bottle
SCREW Lid

SCREW bottom
Lightbulb

SCREW Lid
Jar

Wedges

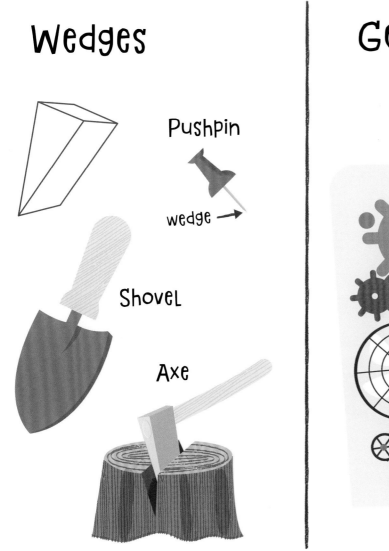

Pushpin

wedge →

Shovel

Axe

Gears

Clock

Machinery

Levers

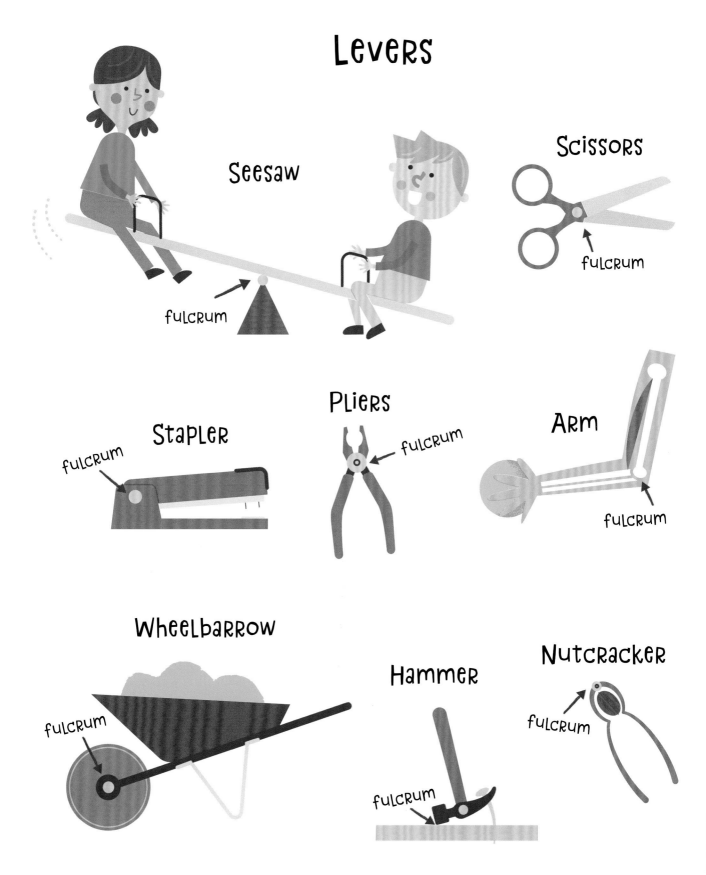

Seesaw

fulcrum

Scissors

fulcrum

Stapler

fulcrum

Pliers

fulcrum

Arm

fulcrum

Wheelbarrow

fulcrum

Hammer

fulcrum

Nutcracker

fulcrum

Pulleys

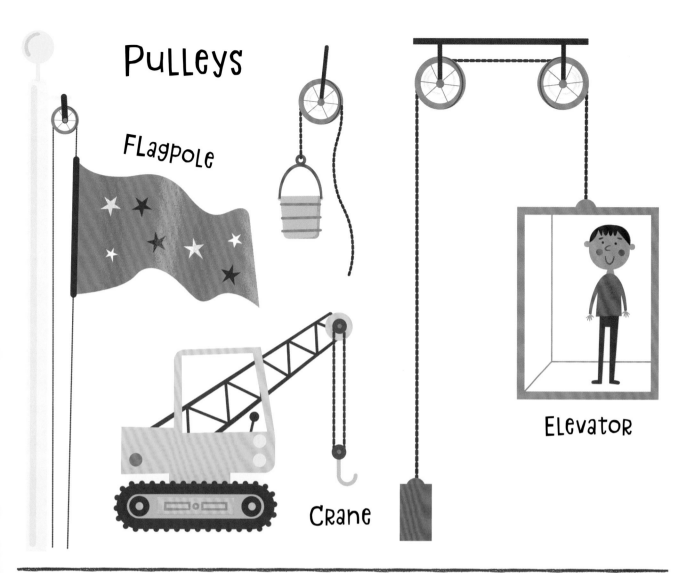

Flagpole

Crane

Elevator

Inclined planes

Ramp

Slide

Library of Congress Cataloging-in-Publication Data

Names: Miller, Edward, 1964- author, illustrator.
Title: Franny's fix-it shop / by Edward Miller.
Description: First edition. | New York : Holiday House, 2022. | Audience:
Ages 6–9. | Audience: Grades 2–3. | Summary: A young girl explains how
simple machines, such as pulleys, wedges, and screws, work as she
repairs her friend's skateboard, the mayor's flagpole, and her
neighbor's scissors.
Identifiers: LCCN 2021027535 | ISBN 9780823443376 (hardcover)
Subjects: CYAC: Simple machines—Fiction. | Repairing—Fiction. | LCGFT:
Picture books.
Classification: LCC PZ7.M61287 Fr 2022 | DDC [E]—dc23
LC record available at https://lccn.loc.gov/2021027535

ISBN: 978-0-8234-4337-6 (hardcover)
ISBN: 978-0-8234-5424-2 (paperback)